CONTEN

Dandelion

A Poem to Share

Written by Hilda Honkling

O little soldier
With the golden helmet,
What are you guarding
On my lawn?

You with your green gun,
And your yellow beard,
Why do you stand so stiff?
There is only the grass to fight!

The Long Grass of Tumbledown Road

Written by Margaret Mahy

Illustrated by Elizabeth Fuller

Tumbledown Road
was a wild road.
Flowers grew tall
between the houses.
Grass grew high
between the houses.

There was a bend
in Tumbledown Road.
"I can't see around
the corner," said
a man driving by.
"Someone must
cut the grass."

The children did not
want Tumbledown Road
to be made too tidy.

They liked walking along
the edge of the road
and making little
caves and forts
in the bushes.

"The grass is too long,"
said the parents.
"Children can't
see cars coming.
Drivers don't know
if there are children
on the edge
of the road."

"I know,"
said a boy
named Brian.
"Let's talk to
Mrs Tumbledown."

10

Mrs Tumbledown
lived at the end
of Tumbledown Road.
She had two goats
and a lot
of other pets.

"I will lend you
my two goats
to eat the grass,"
said Mrs Tumbledown.
"That is plan one!"

"The grass will grow again,"
said the worried parents.

"I will give
each child a present,"
said Mrs Tumbledown.
"That is plan two!"

She gave each child
a guinea pig.
The guinea pigs
loved to eat grass.

Every day before school,
the children ran
up and down
Tumbledown Road,
looking for
guinea pig grass.

The grass grew and grew,
but it never got
a chance to grow
very tall again.

People could drive
down Tumbledown Road.
Children could play
on the edge
of Tumbledown Road.
Guinea pigs had
their breakfast gathered
for them from the edge
of Tumbledown Road.

And up and down
Tumbledown Road,
everyone was happy.

The Plants of My Aunt

Written by Joy Cowley
Illustrated by Elizabeth Fuller

In the house of my aunt,
there were lots and lots
and pots and pots
of plants...

22

plants in the kitchen,
plants in the bathroom,
plants here, plants there,
plants everywhere.

My aunt watered her plants
and talked to them
to make them grow.

"They like my voice,"
she said.

"Don't talk too much," I said.
"They're getting very big."

One day,
I heard a squawking.
I saw a flash of wings.
"Aunt! Aunt!" I said.
"You've got parrots
in your plants...
parrots in the bathroom,
parrots in the kitchen,
parrots here,
parrots there,
parrots everywhere."

"That's nice,"
said my aunt.

The next day,
I heard a pattering
and a chattering.
I saw bright eyes.

"Oh, Aunt! Aunt!
There are monkeys
in your plants...
monkeys here,
monkeys there,
monkeys everywhere."

But my aunt went on
talking to her plants.

A week later, there were plants
out of the windows,
plants up the chimney,
plants through the doors.

I heard a yowling
and a growling.
I saw a striped tail.

"Aunt! Aunt! You've got tigers
in your plants... tigers here,
tigers there, tigers everywhere."

But my aunt didn't answer.
She was nowhere to be seen.

I called the police.
I called the firefighters.
I called the people
from the zoo. They came
with ladders and chainsaws.
They came with cages, too.

They worked all day,
cutting down the plants.
Then they took
the parrots
and the monkeys
and the tigers
to the zoo.

33

The jungle had gone.
Just then,
on the kitchen floor
in a tent, I spied
a sleeping bag
with my aunt inside.

She'd been frightened
by the tigers
and was trying to hide.

"I'm here to rescue you,
dear Aunt!" I cried.

Poor Aunt! She missed
her plants, so I bought her
a plant, a tiny fern in a pot.
"But, Aunt, you are not
to talk to this plant.
Keep it little.
Keep it wee.
Don't say a word to it.
Promise me!"

"I promise,"
said my aunt. "I will
never, never, NEVER
talk to this plant."

It is true.
My aunt
never talks
to her plant,
but, all day long,
she sings
the plant
a little song,
and it grows,
and it *grows*,
and it *grows*,
and it *grows*...

and it *grows*!

The Fox and the Grapes

FROM
AESOP'S FABLES

Illustrated by Xiangyi Mo
and Jingwen Wang

There was once a hungry fox.

One day, he saw some grapes hanging over a high fence.

They looked so good!

The fox jumped
for the lowest
bunch of grapes,
but he could not
reach them.

He jumped again,
and missed
again.

So the fox took
a running start
and jumped
as high as
he could,
but the grapes
were still
out of reach.

The fox kept
trying until
he was tired.

At last, he turned away,
still hungry.

"Those grapes are not worth
one more jump," said the fox.
"I did not want them anyway.
I am sure they are
sour grapes."

Sometimes we pretend that what we cannot get is not worth having.